essenti

Pass Your Practical Driving Test

Time-saving books that teach specific skills to busy people, focusing on what really matters; the things that make a difference – the *essentials*. Other books in the series include:

Making the Most of Your Time

Making the Best Man's Speech

Making Great Presentations

Writing Good Reports

Responding to Stress

Succeeding at Interviews

Solving Problems

Hiring People

Getting Started on the Internet

For full details please send for a free copy of the latest catalogue. See back cover for address.

The things you need to know to

Pass Your Practical Driving Test

David C. Barker

ESSENTIALS

Published in 2000 by
How To Books Ltd, 3 Newtec Place,
Magdalen Road, Oxford OX4 1RE, United Kingdom
Tel: (01865) 793806. Fax: (01865) 248780
email: info@howtobooks.co.uk
http://www.howtobooks.co.uk

First published in 2000
Reprinted in 2001, 2005

British Library Cataloguing in Publication Data.
A catalogue record for this book is available from
the British Library.

Edited by Nikki Read
Cover design by Baseline Arts Ltd, Oxford
Produced for How To Books by Omnipress Ltd
Typeset by PDQ Typesetting, Newcastle-under-Lyme, Staffordshire
Printed and bound by Grafica Veneta in Italy.

NOTE: The material contained in this book is set out in good faith for general
guidance and no liability can be accepted for loss or expense
incurred as a result of relying in particular circumstances on
statements made in the book. The laws and regulations are complex
and liable to change, and readers should check the current position
with the relevant authorities before making personal arrangements.

Contents

Preface

There are many excellent books on learning to drive, written by knowledgeable and qualified driving instructors. What they all have in common is that they stop at the doors to the driving test centre. As an ex-driving instructor and driving examiner I am going to take you through those doors and give you a vital insight into the driving test and the examiners who conduct it.

I will go through each section of the driving test, from arriving at the test centre to the announcing of the decision at the end of the test, and tell you exactly what the examiner will be looking for. I will use actual incidents that happened to me while conducting driving tests. I will explain why some faults are seen as serious and potentially dangerous and result in failure. I will also explain how the examiners reach their pass or fail decision.

As a driving examiner I was frequently asked what the most common reason was for people failing their driving test. Certainly the most commonly marked items on the driving test report sheet are junction observations, hesitancy, reverse observations and mirrors. However, the main reason why people fail their driving test is lack of experience.

Most people want to learn to drive; in fact often they see it as a right, with the driving test as simply an inconvenience standing in the way of their goal. All they really want to do is pass the test, they have no real interest in learning to drive. As a result, and because of the cost, the experience of the candidate is often limited. Yet it is what most often makes the difference between passing and failing. The driving test is, by necessity, becoming harder to pass. The driving test that was introduced in the mid 1930s when roads were quiet and cars rare, could not reflect the skills required to drive on today's crowded, high-speed roads. Gone are the days when you simply had to be 'good enough to be allowed to continue learning without supervision' to pass your test. This meant that you could move off and stop, steer and had a basic understanding of the rules of the road.

Now for you to be issued with that coveted pass certificate you must be confident and competent in all aspects of driving. You must pass a written test on the theory of driving, then you must take the practical driving test and demonstrate for 40 minutes that you can drive without inconveniencing or endangering other road users.

When you do pass the driving test you can be rightly proud of your achievement. It will show that you have demonstrated a high degree of skill and are able to cope with today's demanding driving conditions.

My advice to people learning to drive is:

- Take time selecting a good, professional driving instructor. Shop around and try several before deciding which one you feel more comfortable with.

- Accept that it is going to take you longer as the standard that you have to reach is higher.

- Once you have mastered the basics and feel confident that you can start and stop the vehicle correctly, get a friend or family member to take you out to practise what your instructor has taught you.

- Don't be in a rush to get to the test centre, a little extra time spent polishing the skills you have learnt may save the expense and heartache of a failed test.

David C. Barker

Your Driving Test

The driving test was introduced in the mid 1930s and remained unchanged for almost 50 years. To pass, you had to drive for 20–25 minutes without endangering or inconveniencing other road users. Now you need to be highly skilled in all aspects of driving, from reversing into tight parking spaces to driving at high speed on dual carriageways and motorways. It is no longer practical for new drivers to learn and take their driving test on 30mph urban roads and then 10 minutes after passing their test be able to drive in the rush hour on the M25.

In the last ten years the driving test has been improved to include both driving on crowded urban roads and high-speed multi-lane roads. You will be expected to be able to cope equally well with both. You must be able to demonstrate that you are 'confident and competent' in all aspects of driving. The requirement that other road users have to be endangered or inconvenienced by your actions before you can fail has been removed. Examiners no longer have to give you the benefit of the doubt. If you make a mistake that is 'actually or potentially' dangerous, then you will fail. For example, in the past if you failed to look in your mirror before changing lanes and by sheer luck there was no one there to be inconvenienced, you would have been given the benefit of the doubt. Now, failure to look in the mirror before changing lanes is considered potentially dangerous and will result in you failing. Therefore you must accept that now it is going to take you longer to reach the higher standard to pass your driving test than it would have ten or even five years ago.

This higher standard of driving will hopefully reduce the number of accidents that happen on our roads each year. And as losing your licence for any motoring offence may mean that you have to retake an extended and even more testing driving test, you should think carefully about the way you drive when you eventually throw away those 'L' plates.

THE DRIVING EXAMINER

Driving examiners are selected for their stern, unsmiling appearance, their total lack of any sense of humour and their love of inflicting mental anguish on others. They sit stony-faced, without any hint of emotion while you sweat with terror as you pick your way through the traps that they have laid on the test route to 'catch you out' so that they do not have to issue you with a pass certificate. After all, the only pleasure that they get is telling people that they have failed.

This is the way many people see the driving examiner. Although the 'them and us' situation is slowly changing, driver examiners will always be seen as daunting figures, the enemies, rather than the professionals that they are.

Driving examiners are selected from a wide cross-section of people. What they all have in common is a great deal of driving experience. Most, if not all, will have made their living from driving, in one form or another. Many will be ex-driving instructors, but most of the professional driving careers are represented.

It is true that examiners sit passively during the test, showing little or no emotion. But remember that each examiner does 7 tests each day, 35 tests each week and almost 1700 each year. They have seen drivers who are very good and drivers who are very bad. It is unlikely that you will do anything on your driving test that they have not seen before.

They will not start a conversation with you while you are

driving as they do not wish to distract you from what you are doing. This is also for their own protection, as, in the event of a failure, the candidate could claim that they had been distracted at a vital moment by the examiner speaking to them.

Many examiners will now reply to candidates who wish to talk, as some people find it relieves the pressure of the situation, but they will probably encourage the candidate to concentrate on their driving, rather than discuss the weather.

Senior or supervising examiners constantly monitor driving examiners. These supervising examiners will go out with the examiner on the test, sitting in the back of the car and will mark the candidate's performance. They will not have a say in the result of the test nor will they discuss the test with the candidate. When the examiner and the supervisor return to the office they will go through each individual mark, even minor marks, and the examiner will have to explain why they marked it. The supervisor will then assess the examiner's performance to make sure that they have conducted and marked the test in accordance with DSA policies. Should the supervising examiner feel that the examiner did not conduct the test correctly or that they were over or under marking a certain item, then they can recommend that the examiner is retrained, to bring them back within the guidelines laid down by the DSA.

Do not worry if a supervising examiner comes out on test with you, it will not affect the outcome of your test in any way.

Because of the way examiners are trained and monitored it makes little difference who you get as an examiner, they will all mark your performance the same.

POPULAR MYTHS

I am told that it is quite normal for us, all of us, to transfer blame to others. We do it subconsciously and believe what we say, even though it may not fit the facts. Many urban myths and legends have been built up around the driving test, and people will be happy to tell you their particular variation on a theme. Here are some of the more common, **all of which are untrue.**

- Nobody ever passes on a Friday afternoon.

- Examiners work to strict quotas, and if they have passed their permitted number you will fail, no matter how good you are.

- My instructor said I would have passed with anyone but them, they never pass anyone.

- The examiner put me off by: being miserable, shouting, 'tutting', giving late instructions, not talking, talking too much or one of a hundred other things.

People create and perpetuate myths to avoid being seen as failures or substandard. Don't let other people's horror stories affect your test, just remember:

- **If you are good enough, you will pass.**

1 Requirements of the Eyesight Test

You must be able to comply with the legal requirement for eyesight. You must be able to read a standard number plate at 20.5m (67ft) in good daylight and with the aid of glasses or contact lenses if worn.

The first thing that you will be asked to do is to **read a number plate**. Your examiner will choose one that is well over the required distance. If you cannot read it at this distance, a second number plate will be selected, at roughly the required distance. If you cannot read this one, the examiner will use an official tape measure to measure the exact distance. If you still cannot read the number plate you will fail and the rest of the test will not be conducted. Your examiner would be liable to prosecution if they allowed you to drive knowing that your eyesight was below the legal limit.

If the daylight is poor and could not be described as 'good daylight' the examiner may cancel the test for bad weather i.e. the daylight was not suitable for the eyesight test to be conducted. You will then receive a new test appointment without further charge. This is entirely at the discretion of the examiner and you cannot ask or insist that they cancel the test. If there are other candidates who can read the number plate it is unlikely that this will be an option.

*The candidate had been unable to read the number plate and had been told that he had failed. He produced a letter from his pocket and handed it to me. It was a certificate from an optician that said 'I Dr****** have examined Mr ******** and certify that his eyesight is above that required by law for the driving of a motor vehicle.' I handed it back to him and continued to write out the failure sheet.*

The law says that you must be able to read a standard number plate at the legally required distance at the start of the driving test and if you cannot, you must fail.

TEST TIP

✓ To check your own eyesight, pick a parked car that is too far away to read the number plate. Walk towards it until you can read the numbers clearly. Then continue walking towards it, counting the number of steps. If you are more than 25 steps away your eyesight should be OK. However, if you are less than 25 steps away I suggest you visit an optician.

2 Precautions before Starting the Engine

You must be able to start the engine safely and without assistance or prompting from the examiner. You must be able to disengage steering column locks/immobiliser and know how to operate cylinder heaters on diesel engine vehicles.

At some point in the test your examiner will want to see you **start the engine**. This is to ensure that you know the correct procedure to do it safely, that is without the vehicle rolling or lurching forwards when the starter is operated.

This procedure is usually done outside the test centre at the start of the test, so do not start the engine until your examiner tells you to. Before you operate the starter you must make sure that the handbrake is applied, so that the car is secure, and that neutral is selected.

Most people do this correctly outside the test centre but if they stall the engine while on test, these safety checks are often forgotten in their haste to restart the engine. They may fail to apply the handbrake and the vehicle rolls forwards or backwards as they fiddle with the key. Or they forget to select neutral and the car lurches forwards when the starter is operated. Both of these may be seen as **serious faults** and result in failure.

I had a candidate who stalled the engine because she had tried to move away in third gear. Then instead of putting the handbrake on and selecting neutral, she kept her foot on the brake and depressed the clutch. When she had restarted the engine, she again tried to move away in third gear, stalling the engine. This was repeated on several occasions. Stalling, depressing the clutch to restart, stalling again, until I eventually took pity on the poor car and told her how to correct the fault.

If she had gone through the restart procedure the first time she stalled the engine – handbrake on and select neutral – it is quite probable she would have selected first gear and moved away successfully on the second attempt.

If you do stall the engine while on test, don't panic. Stalling the engine is not usually seen as a serious fault unless it is repeated on several occasions Remember to go through the restart procedure every time and don't turn a minor fault into a failure by forgetting to put the handbrake on or forgetting to select neutral.

TEST TIP

Remember, if you stall the engine:

✓ Put the handbrake on.

✓ Select neutral.

✓ Restart engine.

✓ Go through safety checks again before moving off.

3 Moving Away Safely

You must make all necessary checks to ensure that you do not endanger or inconvenience other road users when moving away from the kerb. You must see and react to the presence of other road users, including pedestrians.

Every time you move away from the kerb, your examiner will watch to make sure that you **complete all the necessary checks** before the handbrake is released.

Most people use the **mirrors** before moving away, so they know exactly what is happening behind them. Unfortunately the same cannot be said about the **blind-spot check** at the side of the car. This is often called the 'life saver' and should be the last check you make before the car starts to move.

The sequence that you should follow to move away from the kerb safely is:

- **Prepare the car**. Make sure you have selected the correct gear and that the engine is running.

- **Look in front of the car**. Check for possible hazards that may affect you as you move away.

- **Look behind the car**. Use all of the mirrors to check for traffic from the rear. Assess whether you can safely move out in front of it.

- **Blind-spot check**. Put your hand on the handbrake ready to release it. Turn your head to the right to check the blind spot is clear. As you head comes back to the front the handbrake should go down and the car start to move.

There should be no delay between the blind-spot check and the car starting to move. It is common for candidates to do the entire pre-move-off checks before they have even put the car into gear. In the time it takes to select the correct gear and prepare to move away the situation can change dramatically. If at any point in the process you decide that it is not safe to move away you must restart the pre-move-off checks again from the beginning.

Your examiner will be looking to see that you:

- do not endanger or inconvenience other road users when moving away

- make all necessary safety checks.

As we moved away after the briefing for the corner reverse exercise, the candidate failed to make the right-shoulder blind-spot check. Fortunately I did. I had to use the dual control brake to stop the vehicle as a youth wearing roller boots had come off the pavement on the right-hand side of the road. He was crossing the road at an angle and was heading to pass just in front of our vehicle. Later the candidate was told that he had failed because I had had to stop the vehicle to prevent a collision. He argued that it was not his fault, as the youth should not have been roller-skating on the public highway. This may or may not be true, but the fact is that he was and the candidate should have seen and reacted to his presence.

TEST TIP

Pre-move-off checks are exactly that, and must be made before the vehicle starts to move.

✓ Prepare the car.

✓ Look in front of and behind the car.

✓ Do the blind-spot check.

4 Moving Away Under Control

You must be able to demonstrate that you can co-ordinate the use of the clutch and accelerator to move the vehicle from rest on level ground and on up-hill and down-hill gradients, without stalling or over-revving the engine.

Moving away from rest is a basic skill required for driving. You must master this before you move on to more advanced parts of the training. When you are first taught to move away, your instructor will teach you to 'set the gas, find the bite point'. This is fine for beginners. However, by the time you get to the driving test centre you must be sufficiently practiced in the use of these controls that they have become 'conditioned action' and do not require conscious thought. If you are still having to think about what your feet are doing when moving away, you need more practice before applying for your driving test.

When moving away, you should not:

- stall the engine
- over-rev the engine
- roll backwards, on up-hill gradients
- lurch forwards as the clutch is released.

Your examiner will be looking to see that you:

- co-ordinate the use of the clutch, accelerator and handbrake
- move away smoothly
- retain full control of the car.

Stalling the engine is not in itself seen as a serious fault, but if it is repeated or there is an obvious fault in your ability to control the vehicle, then it can easily become one. **You will be asked to move away from behind a parked car.** In doing this you will have to co-ordinate the use of clutch, accelerator, handbrake and steer out around the obstruction. You will also have to take extra care with your pre-move-off checks as you may swing out into the path of vehicles in the opposite direction.

You must be able to move away quickly from rest. You will be expected to take advantage of safe gaps in the traffic if they arise and to do so you must be confident in your ability to move away.

From the first time we moved away outside the test centre, I knew it was going to be one those tests. The engine was screaming on almost full revs and the clutch was released with little control, followed by harsh use of the brakes throughout the test. The turn in the road exercise was completed with full engine revs and the distinctive smell of burning clutch lining could be smelt as we finished the exercise. At the end of the test I informed the candidate that he had failed for 'move-off control'. I explained that move-off control meant that he had to demonstrate correct use of the controls, with sympathy for the vehicle, not just apply full engine revs and release the clutch without control.

TEST TIP

✓ Show sympathy for the vehicle in your use of the controls.

✓ Use the same clutch control as you use for the turn in the road exercise when moving out of junctions.

✓ Don't panic if you stall, think about what you have been taught.

5 Using the Controls

You must demonstrate that you can use all of the controls to move, stop and steer your vehicle effectively. Your examiner should not have to assist or prompt you in the operation of the clutch, accelerator, gears, steering, brakes or any of the auxiliary controls that it may become necessary to use to maintain the safety of the vehicle and other road users.

From the first time you get behind the steering wheel of a car to drive, you will be **using the controls**. The **clutch, accelerator, footbrake, handbrake** and **steering wheel** are all part of your first lesson. You will feel awkward at first as it will probably be the first time that you have been asked to use both hands and both feet at the same time. Co-ordination is made harder by the fact that they have to do separate things at the same time.

You will quickly find that things that you may have thought impossible on your first lesson become conditioned actions, i.e. actions that you don't have to think about. Once you have mastered the controls you can move on to other things. However, don't be in too much of a hurry to move on as a little extra time spent on the basics will make you a more competent and confident driver.

Driving examiners have little sympathy for candidates who cannot control their vehicle correctly. By the time you get to the driving test centre you should be sufficiently practiced in the operation of these controls to perform competently throughout the test.

The correct operation of these controls is basic to good driving and any fault or weakness in this area may well be seen as serious and potentially dangerous. Before you move on to, for example, junctions, roundabouts and reversing, ask yourself:

- Am I confident in the way I control the vehicle?

- Is it always under full control?

- Can I retain full control when changing gear or operating the auxiliary controls?

- Does the vehicle always stop where I want it to stop?

If you can answer yes to all of these questions, you are ready to move on to the next stage of learning to drive. If you have any doubts, carry on practising. Your skill in using the controls of your vehicle forms the foundations for your ability to drive. Time spent on this will never be wasted and mastering the controls now may well save you time later in your training.

It was a rainy afternoon and both the candidate and I were wet when we got into the car. Within a very short time of leaving the test centre the windows had misted over. Because I could not see where we were going, I asked the candidate to pull up on the left. As we moved to the left we mounted with both nearside wheels onto the kerb. When we had stopped I asked the candidate if she could see where she was going. I was not surprised when she said that she could not. I then asked if she thought that it was safe to drive when you could not see. She said that it was not safe but that she did not know how to turn the heater on, as her instructor had always operated the controls for her. Although this in itself was not a reason for failing I did invite her to come back and see me again when she had learned how to switch the heater on.

TEST TIP

Before you apply for your test you must be able to:

✓ Operate all the controls smoothly and effectively.

✓ Co-ordinate the use of the clutch, accelerator and handbrake when moving away.

✓ Select the correct gear for the speed you are travelling.

✓ Co-ordinate the use of the clutch and accelerator when changing gear.

✓ Make proper use of the gear box.

✓ Steer a straight course.

✓ Steer effectively when turning corners.

✓ Use the footbrake correctly when stopping.

✓ Use the handbrake, where necessary, when stationary.

✓ Operate any auxiliary controls that may be required, for example, heater blower and heated rear screen.

6 Doing the Emergency Stop Exercise

You must demonstrate that you can stop the car as quickly as possible while retaining full control of your vehicle.

You may or may not be asked to perform an emergency stop, but if you are you must know how to do it correctly. The instruction given will be:

- 'Very shortly I will ask you to stop as in an emergency, the signal will be like this (they will demonstrate the signal to be used). When I do that I want you to stop the vehicle as quickly as possible, as if a child had run off the pavement in front of you. I will have to look behind before the signal is given, so please don't react until I give you the signal to stop.'

Drive normally. Do not drive slowly hoping that the examiner will give the signal at a slow speed. You examiner will normally wait until you are travelling at around 25mph, usually in third gear. Below this speed it would not show if you were doing it correctly.

When the signal is given you must:

- Stop the vehicle as quickly as possible.
- Retain full control of the vehicle.
- Keep the car in a straight line.
- Keep both hands on the steering wheel.

You must not:

- Brake so hard that you lock any of the road wheels.
- Allow the vehicle to skid, either to the left or right.
- Apply the handbrake while the vehicle is moving.
- Depress the clutch pedal before the brake pedal.

On some vehicles with anti-lock brakes the clutch has to be

depressed at the same time the brake is operated, you should check with the operators handbook. Once the vehicle has stopped and the handbrake is applied your examiner will say

- 'I won't ask you to do that exercise again, drive on when you are ready.'

Go through all of your normal move-off checks.

- Check the road in front is clear.
- Check for traffic from the rear (mirrors).
- Right-shoulder blind-spot check.
- Left-shoulder check, to make sure nothing has moved into the gap between your car and the kerb.

You must take the current road conditions into account. If the roads are wet it will take you longer to stop than on dry roads. Your examiner will know this and will take it into account. It is not, however, an excuse not to do an emergency stop, you will be expected to react and stop as quickly as the conditions will allow.

We moved off after the briefing and the candidate accelerated to 25mph, I gave the signal to stop. There was no reaction from the candidate for several seconds and we passed the clear stretch of road I had selected for the exercise. There was now a car parked on the right-hand side of the road and directly opposite it, a tree on the left. I was just about to tell the candidate that the exercise had been aborted, when he hit the brakes, hard. The car skidded violently and turned sideways across the road. There was absolutely nothing I could do, except wait for the crunch. When the car stopped, we were across the road with about a foot or less between our car and the parked car and the tree. The candidate said 'Could I do that again?' My answer was 'Not if you were to try for the text ten years'.

TEST TIP

✓ Make sure that you do the emergency stop exercise with your instructor. Practise the emergency stop until you are confident that you can do it under any road conditions.

7 Corner Reverse Exercise

You will be asked to reverse around a corner, from a major road to a minor road, keeping reasonably close to the left-hand kerb. You must make constant observations throughout the exercise, seeing and reacting to the presence of other road users. You will be asked to reverse to the right if you are driving a van.

For some reason the words 'I'd like you to reverse into this road on the left' strike terror into the hearts of grown men. I have seen candidates who have driven well up to this point, crumble at the thought of reversing around a corner. However, of the three reverse exercises that you can be asked to do, this is probably the easiest.

The words 'reasonably close' give the examiner quite a big margin and how close you will be expected to stay to the kerb will depend on the corner that you are reversing around. If the corner is a large sweeping corner, with a wide radius, then two to three feet from the kerb would be reasonable. If the corner is more severe, perhaps 90 degrees, then it may not be possible to keep within two or three feet and it may be acceptable to go wider. If you do go wider then you will have to get your vehicle back in towards the kerb, as you must finish reasonably close to the kerb, usually within two feet.

Once you have reversed around the corner and are parallel with the kerb, continue to reverse into the side road, until you are told to stop. Your examiner will want to see you reverse in a straight line, parallel to the kerb, for at least two car lengths.

Hitting the kerb is not, as many people think, an automatic failure. The examiner will ask themselves whether you mounted the kerb because you had no idea what you were doing or had lost control of the car. Or, was it a minor error of judgement and did you take the proper action to

27

correct the error?

Your examiner will be looking to see that you:

- Keep the vehicle under control throughout the manoeuvre.

- See and react to the presence of other road users.

- Know which way to turn the steering wheel when going backwards (a surprisingly common fault).

- Keep reasonably close to the kerb.

- Can reverse in a straight line once you are in the side road.

The road that we were reversing into was wide, with sweeping corners, easy to reverse around and excellent visibility. The candidate started to reverse confidently but failed to turn the steering wheel until we were several feet past the point where she should have done and we were well out towards the centre of the road. Then in a panic, she put full left-hand lock on, the car describing a large arc as it gained speed and mounted the kerb with both rear wheels. I had to use the dual controls to stop us hitting the wall. At the end of the test it was no surprise that she had failed. I asked if she always had such a problem reversing. 'No, I can usually do it perfect' was her reply. I asked why she thought she had had so much trouble today. She shook her head and pointed to a row of coloured spots on the rear window. 'Normally I just get that yellow dot lined up on the centre line of the road I'm reversing into, then turn the wheel to the left, hold it there until that blue dot is on the kerb, then straighten it up and keep the blue dot on the kerb. I don't know what went wrong today.'

Using aids such as dots, lines or letters in a sticker in the rear window is common practice for instructors who lack the ability to explain how to reverse correctly. They may work for a particular corner, but cannot work for every corner. In the example above, the road was wider than the one she had practised on and lining up the dot with the centre line put them well out of position.

TEST TIP

✓ You must practise reversing, on different types of corner, until you can judge your distance from the kerb without the need for markers in the rear window.

8 Reverse Parking Exercise

You must be able to park accurately, by reversing either into a parking space on a car park or into a parking space behind another vehicle at the side of the road.

If the driving test centre that you are taking your test at has its own car park you may be asked to **reverse into a car parking space on the car park**. The exercise can be done at the start or the end of the test. You will have the choice of reversing either to the left, right or if there is room, straight back into the space. You will be marked on:

- accuracy
- observations
- judgement.

You must get the vehicle straight and central in the bay and you must judge accurately the distance of the rear of your vehicle with regard to any kerb, marking, barrier or other vehicle.

If you are asked to do the exercise on the road, you will be asked to pull up **alongside and parallel to** a parked vehicle. Then to **reverse back and park reasonably close and parallel to the kerb**. You must complete the exercise within two car lengths of the stationary vehicle. Be careful when moving away from the kerb at the start of the exercise. Remember that you are going to be stopping in the centre of the road so make sure the road is clear behind.

You now have to reverse back and park **reasonably** close, within inches rather than feet, of the kerb. If you need to move forwards to correct your position, one forward manoeuvre is acceptable. When you have finished the exercise ask yourself:

- Am I reasonably close to the kerb?

- Is the vehicle parallel to the kerb?
- Is there no more than one car length between the front of my car and the rear of the other vehicle?
- Would I be happy to lock my vehicle and walk away from it in this position?

When you are practising the reverse park exercise, occasionally get out and have a look, you may be surprised just how far away from the kerb you actually are.

In today's crowded streets with parking spaces at a premium, you will need to be able to reverse park accurately to take advantage of these spaces. Not only will they be considerably less than the two car lengths you get on test but you may also be holding up other motorists as you manoeuvre into them.

TEST TIP

✓ Be careful when moving away from the kerb, remember that you are going to stop in the centre of the road and you do not want to inconvenience following traffic. Make sure there is nothing behind when you move away.

✓ Stop alongside and parallel to the parked car, but don't get too close.

✓ Take careful observations to the rear and front of your vehicle before you start to reverse. You must see and react to other road users.

✓ You do not want to be at an angle of greater than 45 degrees to the kerb. This would cause you to have difficulty getting the front of the car in behind the parked car.

9 Turning in the Road Exercise

You must turn your vehicle around to face the opposite direction, using forward and reverse gear. You must demonstrate a high degree of ability to control the car at a slow speed.

The **turn in the road** exercise is not to see if you can turn the car around. It is to see that you can manoeuvre the car at a slow speed, while steering and watching traffic. It is not *essential* that you get round in three shunts, control of the car is much more important. I have had people take seven shunts and pass, I have also had people take three shunts and fail.

Your examiner will look to see that you:

- Can control the speed of the car by using the clutch.

- Can steer effectively and know which way to turn the steering wheel.

- Can compensate for the camber on the road.

- Retain full control of the vehicle throughout.

- Make proper observations both before and during each leg and react accordingly to other road users.

The candidate presented himself for test in his own car, a large saloon, and the road used for this exercise was relatively narrow. It took the candidate seven shunts to get round. Each shunt was under perfect control and the candidate made good observations before and during each leg. I was happy with his ability to control the vehicle and he passed.

The second candidate, in a driving school vehicle, had little control. The car lurched away from the kerb with high engine revs, getting faster and faster as the candidate struggled to turn the steering wheel. As we neared the kerb she stamped on the brake, throwing me forward violently. With hardly a glance behind, she shot off backwards across the road, still looking forwards and fighting with the steering, again stamping on the brake to avoid the kerb. The third leg was equally exciting, the car being totally out of control, and missing the kerb more by luck than judgement. It was obvious that this person had no control over the car and was invited to come back and see us again.

TEST TIP

✓ The clutch control that you need for the turn in the road exercise is used repeatedly in driving. It is something that you must take the time to master correctly. Once you have mastered it, you will find that reversing, parking and moving in stop–start traffic becomes easier, so it is worth spending some time each lesson practising.

10 Using the Mirrors

You should use your mirrors frequently when driving. You must use your mirrors before you give a signal, change direction, slow down or stop.

Mirror checks should be made frequently during normal driving. They should not cause you to take your eyes off the road in front for any length of time. A quick movement of the eyes is all that is required. If you are not certain of the situation behind then a **series of short glances in the mirror** is preferred to taking your eyes off the road ahead.

If you are changing direction you should use the **interior mirror**, and the **exterior door mirror** appropriate to the direction you are intending to move. Only when you are certain that it is safe and that you are not going to endanger or inconvenience any other road user, should you make your intended manoeuvre. You should use the mirror:

- Before putting your foot on the brake.

- Before indicating.

- Before changing direction, especially on dual carriageways or in multi-lane roundabouts.

- Before accelerating.

- At regular intervals during normal driving.

Planning the road ahead is essential to good driving. You cannot plan the road ahead or the correct action to take unless you know what is happening behind you. The faster you are travelling the earlier and more frequent your mirror checks will need to be.

You may need to make more than one mirror check. If you look in the mirror early in the planning process, as you should, you may need to make several further checks before you can make your manouevre. This will depend on several factors:

- The road on which you are travelling.
- The speed at which you are travelling.
- Other traffic.

Your examiner will be looking to see that you:

- Use the mirror frequently.
- Time the mirror checks correctly before changing speed, direction or giving a signal.
- Make effective use of the information you see in the mirror when planning the road ahead.

We were approaching a roundabout at which I had asked the candidate to turn right. The candidate looked in the mirror, and there was a car travelling a safe distance behind. As we neared the roundabout he could see that there were two lanes on the approach. The candidate looked in the mirror again, and the car that was behind had now gone. The candidate put the right-hand indicator on and immediately started to move to the right. I had to grab the steering wheel and pull it back to the left. The car that had been behind was also turning right and had moved alongside. Had I not pulled the wheel there would almost certainly have been a collision. Although the candidate used the interior mirror correctly, he had made no use at all of the exterior mirrors. A quick glance in the offside door mirror would have shown the overtaking vehicle and this dangerous situation could have been avoided.

If you were travelling in a straight line, at a constant speed you may get away with not looking in the mirror. But if you have to speed up, slow down, change direction, turn, indicate or stop, or if you are approaching anything that may cause you to do any of these, you *must* look in the mirror first.

TEST TIP

Remember:

✓ MIRROR before you do anything.

✓ SIGNAL if you need to.

✓ MANOEUVRE if you are sure it is safe.

11 Giving Signals Correctly

You must give signals that are clear, correct and must not be confusing for other road users. You must give them in good time so that other road users can see and react to them.

As you are no longer required to demonstrate arm signals, **giving signals correctly** should be easy. You flick the switch down to turn left and up to turn right and after you have turned they switch themselves off. Unfortunately it is not quite that simple and many candidates fail for incorrect signals. The most common reasons for failure are:

- Not giving a signal when one is required.
- Failing to cancel a signal after turning.
- Giving a signal too early/late.
- Giving signals other than those approved in the *Highway Code*.

You must give a signal when it will be of benefit to any other road user, including pedestrians. You must not indicate so early that the signal becomes confusing to others, or so late that they do not have time to react to it.

You should be aware that the device that cancels the signal after turning is mechanically operated and will only work if the steering wheel is turned a significant amount, usually more than half a turn. As we only turn the steering wheel a small amount to move in towards or away from the kerb and we may not have to turn it at all to exit a roundabout, the cancelling device may not operate and the signal will remain on. In this case you must remember to cancel the signal manually.

You must not give any signal other than those in the *Highway Code*. You must not flash your headlights to indicate that you are giving way. You must *never* beckon pedestrians to cross the road. Let them decide when it is safe to cross.

If someone gives way to you, a smile and a hand raised in acknowledgements will not be seen as an incorrect signal.

We were driving along a road when the candidate suddenly stopped in the centre of the lane and beckoned a young mother with a pram to cross in front of us. She walked off the kerb and stood in front of our vehicle waiting for a break in the traffic in the opposite direction. Several minutes later we were still waiting and the traffic behind was becoming impatient, with several cars sounding their horns. Eventually a police car in the opposite direction stopped and allowed this young lady to cross. The candidate could not understand why something she thought had shown courtesy and consideration resulted in her failing her test. What she had actually done was invite the pedestrian from a place of safety i.e. the footpath, into a place that was not safe, the centre of a busy main road. In doing so she had seriously inconvenienced several following road users.

TEST TIP

✓ Never give any signal other than those in the *Highway Code.*

✓ Time your signal correctly. Giving a signal too early can be as dangerous as giving it too late or not at all.

✓ Make sure that your signal is correct. For example, if you are indicating left, make sure that you are moving or turning to the left and vice versa.

✓ Make sure that your signal cannot be misunderstood by other road users.

12 Reacting to Road Signs and Markings

You must see and react correctly to all road signs and markings.

At the start of your driving test you will be asked to **follow the road ahead unless traffic signs direct you otherwise**. Your examiner will give you directional information such as, 'at the end of the road turn right', but it is up to you to make sure that it is safe and legal to carry out the instruction. No directional instruction will be given if there is not a choice. If you are at a junction that is a compulsory left turn, denoted by a large blue circle with a white arrow pointing in the direction you have to turn, you will be expected to comply with it, without any prompting by the examiner.

It is common for candidates to miss vital traffic signs, such as compulsory turns, one way street and speed limit changes. Failing to comply with traffic signs is always seen as a serious and potentially dangerous fault.

Make sure that you:

- See *all* traffic signs and road markings.
- Know what they mean.
- Comply with them without prompting.

At the test centre where I worked there was a test route that had a compulsory left turn. It was a 'T' junction and the road that we turned onto was a one way street. I gave no instruction as we approached the junction and the candidate kept looking at me, waiting for me to tell him which way to go. He finally stopped at the give way line, and waited. Eventually he said 'which way?' I pointed to the large blue sign with the white arrow pointing left. 'Do you know what that sign means?' I asked. After looking at it for several seconds he replied 'Yes' and then after a short pause said 'So which way do you want me to go?' I smiled to myself and said 'I think we'd better turn left'.

Can you imagine the chaos this person could have caused if they were allowed to drive in London or Birmingham or any major city? Complicated one way traffic systems mean that you have to see and react instantly to traffic signs and road markings. There can be no excuse for not doing so.

Knowing what a road sign or marking means in a book may be different from knowing what it means to you as a driver.

We were turning right at a set of traffic lights with a yellow painted box junction. The candidate was first in the queue waiting to turn. When the lights went to green, we moved forward but stopped before entering the box junction and waited for the traffic in the opposite direction. The lights changed back to red and then back to green. We continued to wait. Eventually I had to give instruction to get us through the junction. Back at the test centre the candidate gave me the perfect, word for word definition of a box junction from the Highway Code. Unfortunately although they knew what it said, they didn't know what it meant.

TEST TIP

✓ Learn what all road signs mean.

✓ Know how to comply with them correctly.

✓ Get into the habit of looking for them.

✓ If you are unsure of any road sign or marking ask your instructor. They will probably know where they can take you to show you how to treat them correctly when driving.

13 Proper Use of Speed

You must demonstrate that you can judge accurately what is a safe speed to travel at in a given set of circumstances. You must take all of the relevant factors such as weather, road conditions, parked cars and pedestrians into account when deciding how fast you can drive safely.

Just because a road has a speed limit doesn't mean that it is always safe to drive at that speed limit. Although you must always drive within the speed limits, as your examiner cannot condone you breaking the law in any way, you must show that you have sufficient experience to be able to drive at a safe speed, whatever the circumstances. Your examiner will not need to look at the speedometer to see if you are travelling too fast (or too slowly), experience will tell them what is an appropriate speed for the road you are travelling on.

Your examiner will be looking to see that you:

- Take current road conditions into account.
- Drive at a safe speed for those conditions.

Not long after we left the test centre we came to a left-hand bend on a narrow road. On the left a high wall and a tree-lined pavement restricted the view into the bend. To make matters worse a continuous line of parked cars on the right of the road effectively made the road a single track, with nowhere to pass vehicles in the opposite direction. Despite this, the candidate continued to drive at 30mph with little thought for what would happen if a vehicle came in the opposite direction.

At the end of the test he was told that one of the points on which he had failed was driving too fast. He protested that he had driven at the speed limit of 30mph, so how could he have been going too fast. However, in the situation in which he was driving, 20 or even 15mph would have been much safer.

TEST TIP

Knowing 'how fast is too fast' is a skill that will take time and experience to learn. You must not drive unnecessarily slowly but driving too fast for the relevant road conditions is always seen as a serious fault and may result in failure.

When deciding 'how fast is too fast' you should ask yourself:

✓ Can I stop in the distance that I can see to be clear?

✓ If an emergency situation arises, will I have time to react at this speed?

✓ Will the current road conditions mean that I take longer to stop?

14 Making Progress by Avoiding Undue Hesitation

You must demonstrate that you can drive confidently and competently at normal road speeds and that you do not inconvenience other road users by being over-cautious or by over-reacting to minor hazards. Where it is safe and proper to do so, you must keep the flow of traffic moving.

It is important that you keep the flow of traffic moving when it is safe and proper for you to do so. Constantly stopping at junctions when you could safely continue, slowing down for minor or non-existent hazards or driving unnecessarily slowly will seriously inconvenience following traffic. It will also tell the examiner that you are not confident in your own ability.

In today's traffic conditions we cannot sit and wait for roads to be completely clear before moving into traffic. We have to be able to judge when it is safe to move out into a gap or turn across the path of oncoming traffic, without causing them to change speed or direction.

Being able to quickly assess the speed and distance of other traffic is an essential skill of every driver; it will take you considerable time and effort to develop this skill sufficiently. But without it, you cannot be a safe driver.

Your examiner will be looking to see that you:

- Do not endanger other road users by pulling out in front of them, causing them to change speed or direction.

- Do not sit waiting at junctions, allowing safe gaps to pass.

- Do not over-react to minor hazards.

- Do not drive unnecessarily slowly, when it is safe and proper to drive at normal road speeds.

We moved away from the test centre and drove the 200 yards to the junction in first gear. We stopped at every junction and spent a considerable amount of time looking into empty roads waiting for non-existent traffic. On several occasions she selected third gear but the speedometer never reached 20 miles per hour throughout the drive. We covered about one third of the test route. When I told her that one of the points on which she had failed was undue hesitation, she became quite irate. She insisted that it was up to her to decide how fast she wanted to drive and she was adamant that she was going to complain.

A few weeks later she was back in the waiting room; I was pleased that I did not have to take her out this time. As I walked back from my test, she was waiting for me and apologised for her attitude on the previous test. She was in the police force and on returning to the station after the last test had asked a colleague, who was a police class one driver, to take her out to assess her driving and back up her claim against the examiner. The colleague had agreed with me, and said that driving that slowly was totally unacceptable.

TEST TIP

✓ Hesitancy and junction observations often go hand in hand on failure sheets. They are both caused by an inability to judge how far away a vehicle is and how fast it is travelling. Do not take your test until you are confident that you are able to assess quickly the speed and distance of other traffic.

15 Following Behind Other Vehicles Safely

You must maintain a safe separation gap between you and the vehicle in front. You must react promptly to any change in speed of the other vehicle.

When you are travelling behind another vehicle you must make sure that you leave sufficient room to stop safely, if the other vehicle were to stop suddenly. The **two second rule** is the usual method that examiners use to decide if you are too close to the car in front, but if the roads are wet this distance must be increased.

Travelling too close behind another vehicle is very dangerous, as it gives you very little time to react should the unexpected happen. Although the examiner will give you a short time to adjust your distance from the vehicle in front, it will only be a few seconds. Their life is at risk, as well as yours, and they will very soon be asking you to increase the distance between you and the vehicle in front.

It is a requirement of law that you travel at a speed so that you can stop **within the distance that you can see to be clear**. There can be no excuse for running into the rear of another vehicle, even if the other vehicle stops suddenly and without warning.

If you are stopping in traffic behind another vehicle, you must maintain a safe gap. You should not get too close to the rear of the vehicle in front. Instructors use many different methods for teaching separation gaps when stationary. I personally used to get pupils to leave enough room so that if the vehicle in front broke down, they could still move out around it.

The candidate had been driving in stop-start traffic for some minutes without a problem, keeping a good gap from the car in front. The car in front then turned off and left us following an articulated lorry and trailer. The first time the lorry stopped, I realised that we were going to go under the back of the trailer and I had to use the dual controls to stop us. At the end of the test I asked why they had not stopped further back away from the trailer 'My instructor told that when I stopped in traffic I should underline the back wheels of the vehicle in front with the bonnet of my car'. This method of teaching separation in stationary traffic works fine on cars but lorry trailers often have overhangs that can be ten or twelve feet from the wheel to the end of the trailer. Common sense should have told this candidate that if you were actually under the trailer you were too close.

TEST TIP

Make sure that you:

✓ Use the two second rule to make sure you maintain a safe gap, especially on high-speed roads.

✓ React promptly to the vehicle in front slowing down. Do not allow the gap to diminish before you start slowing down.

✓ Do not get too close before moving out to overtake.

16 Junction Positioning

You must position at junction so that, where possible, you do not prevent other vehicles from taking up their position. You must take all relevant factors into account when deciding where the correct position is for the turn that you wish to make.

If the roads are clear and there are no other factors to be taken into account positioning is easy. To position to turn right, you should move as far to the right as you safely can, that is, a few inches left of the centre line. To turn left, you move as far to the left as you safely can, following the line of the kerb where possible. However, other factors can make selecting the correct position more difficult.

- parked cars
- road works
- pedestrians
- other vehicles.

You must decide on the most practical place to position so that you do not inconvenience other road users. For example, normally when turning right from major road to minor road you would position with your offside wheels against the centre of the road, far enough forward to see clearly into the road you are turning into. However, if there was a vehicle parked near the junction and by taking up this position you would prevent traffic in the opposite direction from passing, you may be expected to position well to the left. This will allow traffic to continue and prevent a grid lock situation arising. Although most textbooks will tell you to turn offside to offside, it is now generally accepted that nearside to nearside is the better option at most junctions. You should know both methods of turning and use the one most appropriate to the situation at the time.

Your examiner will be looking to see that you:

- Plan the junction as you approach it.

- See any hazards that may affect where you position.

- Choose the correct position after taking all relevant factors into account.

I had asked the candidate to turn right from a major road. In the opposite direction and already positioned to turn right, was a large articulated vehicle. Instead of waiting for the lorry to turn across our path, the candidate continued into the junction and attempted a hook turn. We now had a situation where the lorry could not turn because there was not enough room, and we could not turn because it was blocking our path. This candidate had been taught that you must turn offside to offside and had stuck to this rigidly. In driving, as with most things in life, common sense sometimes has to be used.

TEST TIP

Make sure that you:

✓ Plan every junction. You may have been through this junction a hundred times but a parked car may alter where you should position this time.

✓ Look out for traffic signs and road markings, they may tell you where you should position.

✓ Use common sense when deciding where to position.

17 Junction Observations

You must be able to judge both speed and distance of approaching vehicles. You must take advantage of safe gaps in the traffic but you must not cause any other road user to change speed or direction because of your actions.

The ability to judge the speed of other vehicles is essential to good driving. Until you have mastered this skill you cannot hope to drive safely. If you cannot judge speed and distance it will be obvious in one of two areas.

- You will sit at junctions, allowing safe gaps to pass, holding up following traffic. This will be marked as hesitancy.

- You will pull out into traffic and cause other road users to change their speed or alter their direction to avoid a collision.

Both of these show that you have not yet developed the necessary skills to judge when it is safe for you to continue. They are always seen as serious and potentially dangerous faults.

Your examiner will be looking to see that you:

- Make good observations, in all directions, before emerging.

- Assess the speed of other vehicles accurately.

- Take advantage of safe gaps as they arise.

- Do not cause other vehicles to change speed or direction by your actions.

We were waiting to emerge from a side road on to a 40mph, single carriageway road. To our right a considerable distance away, there was a vehicle approaching. It was obviously travelling at high speed, well over the speed limit. The candidate started to move out and I operated the dual brake. Within two or three seconds this other vehicle passed. Even if we had moved out, the other vehicle would have had to swerve or brake hard to avoid us. The candidate said that I was being unfair by failing them, as it was the other driver that was at fault by driving so fast. Unfortunately 'it was the other driver's fault' could be the epitaph on many gravestones. You must assess the situation and react to things as they actually are and not how they should be.

TEST TIP

✓ Practise judgement of speed and distance whenever possible, especially when travelling as a passenger.

✓ Once you have decided that there is a safe gap, be confident and accelerate briskly into the flow of traffic.

✓ Look both ways before emerging as the road must be clear in both directions.

✓ Watch out for pedestrians who may be crossing or about to cross the road.

18 Meeting, Overtaking and Crossing the Path of Other Vehicles

You must be able to judge the speed of approaching vehicles and plan the road ahead so that you do not cause other vehicles to take evasive action if you meet at a restriction in the road or you turn across their path. You must know how to overtake a moving vehicle safely.

At some point on your test you will almost certainly come to a **restriction in the road**. This will usually be a parked vehicle, which will reduce the width of the road to single file. You must plan your approach and be prepared to slow down or stop if necessary. If the obstruction is on your side of the road the onus is on you to stop. If it is on the other side of the road, then the driver in the opposite direction should stop. However, do not assume that the other driver will stop just because they should. If there is a line of parked cars on the right and a vehicle in the other direction is already in the hazard, there is no point in you continuing into it.

Your examiner will be looking to see that you:

- Plan the situation early, the earlier you react, the less severe the action you have to take.

- Take appropriate action, slowing down or stopping if necessary.

- Give way to vehicles already in the hazard.

- Negotiate the hazard safely.

The hazard, a parked car, was on our side of the road. There was a car in the opposite direction that was slightly farther away from the obstruction than we were. The candidate made no attempt to slow down or stop but continued to pass the parked car. The car in the other direction had to brake hard to avoid a collision. The candidate made matters worse by smiling at the other driver and putting a hand up to thank them. A string of mouthed expletives and a very different hand signal was the answer. At the end of the test I informed the candidate they he had failed because of the 'meet' situation. He replied that it was up to the other driver to stop because they had reached the parked car first. I explained that unless you can pass the hazard and move back to your side of the road without causing the other vehicle to change speed or direction, then it is up to you to take avoiding action.

Turning right across the path of approaching traffic is probably the most dangerous exercise you will have to perform when driving. In today's driving conditions, with crowded roads, you cannot afford the luxury of waiting for the road to be completely clear.

You must be able to:

- Judge the distance of the approaching vehicle.
- Judge the speed of the approaching vehicle.
- Move away and turn quickly.

If the vehicle has to slow down or alter its course by even a small amount because of your actions, it will be seen as a serious and potentially dangerous fault.

When waiting to turn right the car should be set up and ready to move quickly when a safe gap occurs. The correct gear should be engaged and although the handbrake should be on, you should keep your hand on it ready to release it.

You will be expected to **overtake slower vehicles** if there is an opportunity to do so safely. You must:

- Select a safe place.
- Take effective observations.

- Select the correct gear to give maximum acceleration for the speed you are travelling.

- Complete the manoeuvre quickly.

We had been following the tractor for some considerable time, when an opportunity to pass it presented itself. It was a long straight road with no turnings off and no visible traffic in the opposite direction. The candidate made good rear observations and moved out to overtake. Unfortunately we were in fourth gear and travelling at less than 20 mph. As we accelerated slowly I was concerned about how close we were getting to the bend. Suddenly a car came around the bend towards us. As we now didn't have enough room to get past the tractor, I had to use the dual brake to slow us down and move back in behind it. Had the candidate selected the correct gear, third or even second gear at the speed we were travelling, he would have had the acceleration to pass quickly and safely.

TEST TIP

When meeting other vehicles:

✓ See and react to potential hazards early.

✓ Don't race vehicles in the opposite direction, be prepared to give way even if technically you have the right of way.

✓ Be certain that there is enough room for two before you commit yourself to going into a tight gap. The gap may look wider than it actually is.

When overtaking:

✓ Don't overtake unless you can pass the vehicle and get back to your side of the road in the distance you can see to be clear.

✓ Use your mirrors and indicate before pulling out.

✓ Make sure you have selected a gear that will give you the acceleration to pass the other vehicle quickly.

When crossing the path of other vehicles:

✓ Be ready to move when there is a safe gap.

✓ Check that the road you are turning into is clear before you commit yourself to turning.

✓ Do not cause other vehicles to change speed or direction as you turn.

✓ Accelerate briskly across the road, but not so fast that you lose control.

19 Approaching Pedestrian Crossings

You must demonstrate courtesy and consideration for people waiting to cross the road at pedestrian crossings. You must give way to them when it is obvious that they intend to cross the road.

There will be **pedestrian crossings** on your test route, probably several and of different types. You must see and react to them all correctly. There are four main types of pedestrian crossings:

- **Zebra crossings**. Black and white stripes across the road and flashing yellow lights on black and white striped poles on the footpath at each side. Pedestrians waiting to cross the road have right of way and you must stop and give way to them. They do not have to put their foot on the crossing as they once did, as long as it is obvious that they wish to cross the road. (A mother pushing a pram would not be able to put her foot on the crossing without pushing the pram into the road first.)

- **Pelican crossings**. Or **Pe**destrian **Light Con**trolled crossings. These are operated by the pedestrian pressing a button and causing traffic lights to change to red, stopping the traffic. When the red light changes to amber, the amber light will flash. While the amber light is flashing pedestrians who are already on the crossing have right of way and you must wait. If the crossing is clear, you should continue even though the amber light is still flashing.

- **Puffin crossings**. **P**edestrian **U**ser **F**riendly crossings. Operated exactly the same by the pedestrian but there is no flashing amber light for the driver. Instead a sensor keeps the red light showing while there is movement on the crossing. Once the crossing is clear the lights will change to amber and green as would standard traffic lights and should be treated the same.

- **Toucan crossings**. They are exactly the same in operation for both pedestrian and driver as the Puffin crossings. They are situated where both footpath and cycle track cross a road and **TwO CAN** cross at the same time, the two being cyclists and pedestrians. Cyclists do not have to dismount to cross at these crossings.

All pedestrian crossings have zigzag white lines painted in the kerb and centre of the road. You should not park or allow your vehicle to stand within the confines of the crossing, marked by the zigzag lines, unless you are:

- in a line of stationary traffic
- stopping to allow pedestrians to cross the road.

You must never:

- Overtake the lead vehicle that has stopped at pedestrian crossings, even on dual carriageways, as they may be preventing you from seeing people already on the crossing.

- Stop with your vehicle wholly or partly blocking the crossing.

- Harass people on the crossing by revving your engine or moving forward as they cross.

We were moving slowly forwards in stop-start traffic, the candidate intent on keeping up with vehicle in front as it moved forward. The driver of the vehicle allowed a gap of two to three car lengths before he moved and without looking the candidate immediately released the handbrake and followed. Unfortunately the candidate had not noticed that the other driver had waited because there was a pedestrian crossing and had wanted to be able to clear the crossing. The candidate in his haste had moved onto the crossing but was unable to clear it, therefore completely blocking the crossing. As we stopped, the pedestrian crossing signal could be heard and people started to walk both in front of and behind our vehicle. To make matters worse, a person with a guide dog crossed from the right. The dog, trained to stay on the crossing, stood waiting for the crossing to clear. Fortunately a pedestrian saw what was happening and assisted the blind person and the dog safely to the other pavement.

TEST TIP

✓ See and plan pedestrian crossings as early as possible.

✓ Be prepared to give way to anyone who looks like they are intending to cross the road. Remember that a mother with a pram or pushchair would not be able to step onto the crossing without first pushing the pram onto the crossing, endangering the child. If it is obvious that they wish to cross the road, stop.

✓ Be especially careful at crossings that are close to junctions or roundabouts. Your attention may be distracted by the junction and you may not see people on the crossing or waiting to cross.

20 Selecting Places for Normal Stops

You must select places to stop your vehicle that are safe, convenient and legal.

You will be asked several times to **pull in on the left in a convenient place** during the course of the test. Although on occasions your examiner will specify where they want you to stop, for example, 'before you get to the next road on the left', it will usually be left to you to decide where. There are three questions that you should ask yourself before you select a place to stop:

- Is it safe?
- Is it convenient?
- Is it legal?

Parking too close to a junction may be considered unsafe, as you will restrict other road users being able to see into the road. **Parking opposite a 'T' junction** may be considered unsafe, as you will force passing vehicles to be on the wrong side of the road when passing the junction.

Parking across driveways, entrances or too close to other parked vehicles may be inconvenient, as you may prevent other road users from using the entrance or from moving away.

Double yellow lines, zigzag lines outside schools or at pedestrian crossings, bus stops or anywhere where parking is restricted or prohibited are places where you must not stop, as you would be committing an offence.

TEST TIP

✓ Stop as soon as it is safe for you to do so, do not continue to drive for a long distance once you have been asked to stop. Try and stop at the first safe and convenient place that you come to.

21 Allowing Adequate Clearance of Stationary Vehicles

You must give stationary vehicles sufficient clearance so that if anything unexpected happens, you have time and room to take evasive action.

As a driving examiner my pet hate was hurtling down the road only inches away from parked cars. I'm sure that if you asked other driving examiners they would tell you the same. It can be very unnerving sitting waiting for the wing mirrors to collide, especially when there is ample road width for the candidate to give a safe clearance.

You should give enough room for the car door to open or at least three feet. If, as you often will, you have to get closer to the parked car than this you must adjust your speed accordingly. The nearer you get, the slower you must go.

Your examiner will look to see that you:

- Maintain a safe gap when passing parked cars.

- Reduce your speed if you have to reduce the safety gap between you and the parked cars.

We had been driving much too close to the parked cars since the test had begun. We were passing a long line of parked cars, with only inches between our nearside mirror and the parked cars offside mirrors. One of the parked cars was sticking out a few inches further than the others. The candidate made no attempt to move out and the wing mirrors hit. Both wing mirrors were broken. The candidate failed and the test was terminated then and there, as the vehicle was no longer suitable for conducting a driving test. It had been a wide main road, with no traffic in the opposite direction. There was ample room for the candidate to have given ten feet of clearance to the parked car, without crossing the centre line of the road.

TEST TIP

Always remember:

✓ Keep away from parked cars.

✓ Give parked cars at least three feet clearance.

✓ The nearer you get, the slower you must go.

22 Anticipating the Actions of Other Road Users

You must plan the road ahead of you and anticipate what other vehicles and road users may do.

Being able to **anticipate** what others may do, by looking at what is happening now and using your experience to 'guess' what may happen next, is a very difficult skill to learn. It is almost impossible to teach, although good instructors will start pointing out potential hazards ahead. Only experience will allow you to anticipate others effectively.

Your examiner will be looking to see that you:

- 'Read' the road ahead, and use the information to plan your actions.

- Anticipate what other motorists may do and react accordingly.

We were travelling along a road and some distance in front a large articulated lorry had pulled into a road on the right but had stopped with the back of its trailer still blocking the right-hand half of the road. Opposite the road the lorry was in was a gateway to a factory. There was ample room for us to pass behind the lorry and the candidate continued without any safety checks or reduction in speed. As we neared the trailer, it was obvious that the reverse lights were on, but the candidate still continued. Suddenly the lorry started to reverse, and as we were now quite close I had to use the dual brake to stop us from going into a dangerous situation. At the end of the test the candidate complained bitterly that it was the lorry driver's fault for reversing when they could not see that it was safe.

I could not argue with that, but all the clues indicated that it was going to happen:

- lorry half in the road
- factory gates directly opposite
- reverse lights on.

These clues should have told the candidate that there was a distinct possibility that this vehicle was going to reverse across in front of us and they should take appropriate action.

TEST TIP

✓ Always look for 'clues' as to what may happen and never expect people to do what they are supposed to do, or even what they are indicating they are going to do, until they actually do it.

23 Negotiating Roundabouts

You must demonstrate that you know the correct procedure at roundabouts. You must take up the correct position on approach and in good time. You must maintain the correct course on the roundabout and make good use of mirrors and signals.

Roundabouts are becoming more and more common on today's roads. Large multi-lane roundabouts are frequently used at busy junctions or where high-speed roads cross. As the test has been extended to allow for longer test routes, it is almost certain that you will be expected to cope with one at some point in your driving test.

Your examiner will be looking to see that you:

- Know which lane to use for the direction you are going.

- Take up your position in good time.

- Use the mirror, signals, manouevre (MSM) routine when changing lanes.

- Take advantage of safe gaps when entering the roundabout.

- Select and maintain the correct lane in the roundabout.

- Make frequent and effective use of mirrors.

- Clear the junction as quickly as possible.

Traffic may be moving at quite high speed on the approach to and when on roundabouts. It is essential that you can judge the speed and distance of approaching vehicles accurately and that you can move away and accelerate quickly while retaining full control.

It may be daunting at first to find yourself waiting at roundabouts with traffic on both sides of your vehicle, but with practice you will soon get used to this. Remember that lanes in roundabouts may not be marked with white lines,

but they are still there, and you will be expected to follow
the correct course and use the MSM routine before altering
your position in the roundabout.

*We were returning to the test centre after what had been a good
drive and the candidate was going to pass. A short distance from the
test centre there was a large roundabout, with four lanes on the
approach. I asked the candidate to turn right. He used the MSM
routine correctly and positioned correctly in the right-hand lane. He
(and I) looked to the right. There was a double-decker bus almost in
the roundabout and travelling at high speed. I expected the
candidate to stop. Instead he changed into second and went to
accelerate into the roundabout. Instinctively I hit the dual controls to
stop us as the bus missed the front of our car by inches. I was
surprised that after such a good drive he had made such a
dangerous error. At the test centre I asked him what he had been
thinking about and with a deadly serious face he said 'I thought it
was a number 74'. When I asked what difference the bus's route
number made, he said 'if it had been a number 74, it would have
turned left at that roundabout'.*

TEST TIP

Before you take your driving test you must:

✓ Know where to position and have the confidence to take up this position in good time.

✓ Know the correct line to take through the roundabout, so that you do not endanger or inconvenience other road users.

✓ Know the correct procedure for mirrors and signals, when entering and exiting roundabouts.

✓ Be able to judge accurately speed and distance of approaching traffic.

24 High Speed Driving

You must be able to demonstrate that you can control your vehicle at all speeds, including de-restricted and high-speed roads, where practical. You must drive at or near the indicated speed limit, or as fast as it is safe to do, so taking relevant road and traffic conditions into account.

Driving on today's roads means driving faster. Many ordinary main roads have 40, 50 or even 60 miles per hour speed limits. Motorways may have several lanes and complex junctions with their own set of rules and problems. It is impossible, therefore, to drive on today's roads without encountering high-speed traffic. Because of this the driving test has been extended to allow higher speed roads to be included in the test route and it is almost certain that at some point on your test you will be expected to drive on one of these high speed roads.

Your examiner will be looking to see that:

- You can drive confidently and competently at these higher speeds.

- You take the relevant road and traffic conditions into account when deciding on a safe speed.

- You take the higher speed and therefore the longer stopping distances into account when planning the road ahead.

- You use the footbrake correctly when slowing down.

- You use the mirror effectively.

- You make proper use of any acceleration or deceleration lanes that may be available.

When driving on multi-lane carriageways remember that you may have traffic on both sides of your vehicle and that you may not be able to see them in the interior or exterior

mirrors. You may have to turn your head to check that there
are no vehicles in the blind spots before changing lanes
(motor cycles can easily be missed). This blind-spot check
should take no more than a fraction of a second and you
will need to practise it, as the movement may cause you to
swerve.

The mirror should be used more frequently and it should
be remembered that vehicles seen in your exterior mirrors
might be closer than they look. Convex glass is often used
in exterior mirrors and although this gives a wider field of
vision, it makes vehicles look farther away then they actually
are.

Signals should be given in good time. Remember that
putting a signal on does not give you the right to move
across the lanes, it only tells other road users that you wish
to do so. You must not cause others to change speed or
direction. Remember that traffic that may seem a long way
back may be moving fast and could overtake you in only a
few seconds. Make sure that you can make your manoeuvre
without inconveniencing or endangering it.

Your use of all the controls needs to be smooth and
progressive. Any sudden or jerky movement of the steering
wheel may cause the vehicle to veer violently and become
uncontrollable. Harsh braking from high speed will cause
the vehicle to skid unless the braking process is controlled
correctly. The pressure applied to the brake pedal should be
progressive, steadily increasing until the required braking
pattern is achieved. As the vehicle slows, the pressure on
the brake pedal should be released, so that the braking
effect is constant throughout the stopping process. Wet or
icy roads will increase the chances of the car going out of
control if the controls are operated incorrectly.

Even on dry roads you should avoid braking on bends

when travelling at high speed. Centrifugal force and inertia will cause the weight of the vehicle to be transferred onto the front wheel on the outside of the bend and may cause the vehicle to skid. Once a vehicle has started to skid in this fashion it usually results in the vehicle spinning uncontrollably, often with disastrous results.

Motorways are high-speed roads and are amongst the safest roads to travel on. All of the traffic is going in the same direction, at similar speeds and there are no junctions or traffic lights to cause you to stop. When driving on the motorway you should:

- Drive at or near the speed limit. Remember that driving too slowly or too fast can be equally as dangerous. Make sure that you know the speed limit for your vehicle and the limitations that are placed upon it when driving on the motorway.

- Use the 'two second rule' to maintain a minimum gap at all times. If another vehicle moves into your safety gap drop back, using your mirrors first to make sure that you can do so safely, and reinstate your safety zone.

- React early to vehicles in front changing their speed; use your footbrake to maintain the safety gap. Don't wait until you have to brake hard to avoid running into the back of the vehicle in front.

- Watch out for vehicles entering the motorway from acceleration lanes on the left (occasionally these slip roads may be on the right). If you see a vehicle approaching the motorway, and you can do so safely, move into the centre lane and allow it to enter the main carriageway.

- Do not slow down on the main carriageway before

leaving the motorway. Maintain your speed until you have moved into the deceleration lane.

As a learner driver you are prohibited from driving on the motorway. Your examiner cannot take you onto the motorway as part of your driving test. But your test route will almost certainly contain a section of de-restricted or high-speed road. Most, if not all test centres will have suitable dual carriageways for testing your ability to drive at high speed.

TEST TIP

✓ Where road and traffic conditions allow, accelerate briskly when joining high-speed roads. Use the acceleration lane to match your speed to that of the traffic already on the high-speed road.

✓ If you are turning from a side road onto a high-speed road always accelerate up to the speed limit as quickly as you safely can. Remember that vehicles that may be a long way off as you pull out will soon be slowing down behind you unless you accelerate up to the speed limit.

✓ Use your mirrors frequently. It is essential that you know at all times what is happening behind you. Be especially careful when changing lanes or slowing down. Situations can change very quickly at these speeds.

✓ React quickly to the traffic in front of you slowing down. As soon as the brake lights come on on the vehicle in front, use your mirrors and slow down to maintain the safety gap. If not, you will very quickly catch up with the vehicle in front and find yourself having to brake hard to try to avoid running into the back of it.

✓ Plan early for junctions, traffic lights etc. Slow down in a controlled and progressive way and avoid sudden or harsh use of the controls.

✓ Remain within the speed limit for your vehicle at all times.

At the End of the Test

At the end of your driving test your examiner will have a decision to make. Usually this decision is easy, because you, by your driving, will have made it for them. Most tests result in a definite pass or fail and you will (if you are honest with yourself) have a good idea which it is. Some tests, however, are less 'black and white' and the examiner will have to use their skill and judgement to make a decision.

All test decisions are reached by the examiner looking at your overall performance, your strengths and your weaknesses and by asking themselves whether this person is capable of driving on the public highway without endangering themselves and others: can they control their vehicle under all conditions and do they understand the rules of the road? If the answer to any of these question is 'no' then you must fail.

Hopefully at the end of your test your examiner will say: 'That is the end of the test and I'm pleased to tell you that you have passed. Could I see your driving licence again please.' They will then transfer the details from your provisional licence onto the certificate of competence and ask you to sign it. Once the certificate is signed it gives you all the rights of a qualified driver. You can drive without displaying 'L' plates, without supervision and you can drive on the motorway. You should send the pass certificate to the DVLA as soon as possible and they will send you your full driving licence.

Remember that you cannot supervise a learner driver unless you are over 21 years of age and have held a full licence for three years.

If you are unsuccessful your examiner will say: 'That is the end of the test and I'm sorry your driving has not reached the required standard. If you give me a few moments I'll go through the main points with you.'

You will probably be very upset at this point but try to listen to what the examiner has to say. They will highlight the areas that were unacceptable and why. Although they will give specific areas in which you need to improve, you should not think that these are the only things that you need to practise. Your examiner will not give you instruction on how to correct the faults they highlight, that is your instructor's job.

Pass or fail your examiner will not reach their decision lightly. You will only fail if you have a flaw in your driving that may cause you to be a danger to yourself and the general public. You must accept that it is your performance on the day that determines the result.

You could take another test the same day, if a test slot is available, but this isn't recommended. It is much better to spend some time correcting the failure points and generally improving your driving skills before taking the test again.

People who want to learn to drive properly and work hard learning both the theory of driving as well as the practical side of driving, usually make better, safer drivers and find passing the driving test easier than those whose only interest is passing the driving test.

Driving any vehicle is a great responsibility. You are responsible not only for your own safety and that of your passengers, but for the safety of every other road user that you meet, whether they are drivers, cyclists or pedestrians.

Once you have passed your test think carefully about post-test training. Motorway driving, night driving and advanced driving courses are available and will improve your driving skills considerably.

Disabled Drivers

Many people with disabilities learn to drive. Despite or perhaps because they have to work harder to overcome their particular disability as well as learning to drive, the standard of driving is usually high. If you have a disability you should declare it on the application form when you apply for your test. More time is allowed for disability tests, not only because it may take a disabled person more time to get to and from the waiting room but also because there is more paperwork for the examiner at the end of the test. If you have a severe walking problem, stay in the car, get your accompanying driver to go into the waiting room and tell your examiner where you are, they will then come out to the car.

Adaptations may be fitted to your vehicle to enable you to overcome the effects of your disability. These may be simple or complex, depending on the nature of your disability.

The test itself is exactly the same as a standard driving test, no reduction in standards is acceptable. There are several disabled drivers' clubs recommended by the DSA who will advise disabled drivers on what adaptations are available to them. Details of these organisations can be found in any driving test centre. If you take and pass your driving test with adaptations fitted to your vehicle, such as extra blind-spot mirrors, steering balls, hand-operated accelerator and brake, you must only drive vehicles with these adaptations or you will be committing a driving offence and liable to prosecution. When you pass, your certificate will be annotated 'with controls adapted to suit disability'. The examiner will then list all the adaptations that were fitted to your vehicle and they will be included in the form that is sent to the medical branch of the licensing authority.

Even if you have a disability that you think does not affect your driving ability, it should still be included on the application form. I once had a candidate who had lost the fingers of his right hand in an accident. Because it was not listed on my programme as a disability test I asked whether it had been declared on the application. The candidate said that it had not as it did not affect his ability to drive. This was true and he passed the test. I then asked him if he could ride a motor cycle, as it would require him to operate the handbrake with his right hand. He said that he could not. I then had to explain that by passing the group B test for a motor car, it also gave him the entitlement to ride a moped, which have hand-operated brakes. I then annotated his pass certificate 'vehicles in group B only'. This effectively removed his entitlement to drive or ride vehicles in any other group.